better together*

*This book is best read together, grownup and kid.

a
kids
book
about

a kids book about mindfulness

by Caverly Morgan

A Kids Co.
Editor Denise Morales Soto
Designer Duke Stebbins
Creative Director Rick DeLucco
Studio Manager Kenya Feldes
Sales Director Melanie Wilkins
Head of Books Jennifer Goldstein
CEO and Founder Jelani Memory

DK
Editor Emma Roberts
Senior Production Editor Jennifer Murray
Senior Production Controller Louise Minihane
Senior Acquisitions Editor Katy Flint
Acquisitions Project Editor Sara Forster
Managing Art Editor Vicky Short
Publishing Director Mark Searle
DK would like to thank Dr Sharie Coombes

This American Edition, 2024
Published in the United States by DK Publishing
1745 Broadway, 20th Floor, New York, NY 10019

DK, a Division of Penguin Random House LLC
Text and design copyright © 2020 by Caverly Morgan.
A Kids Book About, Kids Are Ready, and the colophon 'a' are trademarks of A Kids Book About, Inc.
24 25 26 27   10 9 8 7 6 5 4 3 2 1
001-339423-July/2024

A catalog record for this book is available from the Library of Congress.
ISBN: 978-0-7440-9897-6

DK books are available at special discounts when purchased in bulk for
sales promotions, premiums, fund-raising, or educational use. For details, contact:
DK Publishing Special Markets, 1745 Broadway, 20th Floor, New York, NY 10019, or SpecialSales@dk.com

Printed and bound in China

www.dk.com

akidsco.com

MIX
Paper | Supporting
responsible forestry
FSC™ C018179

This book was made with Forest
Stewardship Council™ certified
paper – one small step in DK's
commitment to a sustainable future.
Learn more at www.dk.com/uk/
information/sustainability

For Rupert Spira.

Your support for me, and the work of Peace in Schools, has been invaluable. Thank you for all that you give and for your precise and loving articulation of Truth.

Intro
for grownups

We are human beings. *Homo sapiens*. *Homo* means human. *Sapiens* means wise. In the modern world, with its endless distractions, we easily forget our roots. We are habituated to turn our attention outward—most, if not all of the time. For millennia, Indigenous cultures across the planet have nurtured ways to know our inherent wisdom.

Globally, our ancestors discovered how to be mindful—to awaken, to love, to value and integrate difference, to be just, and to honor the land. Today, modern science is validating the wisdom that humans throughout time have discovered by turning inward.

This book is an invitation to you, and the kid you're reading with, to discover, to reconnect with, and to remember the heart of our being. The heart of all beings.

This book reminds us that all being is shared being. To know this is peace. To live this is love.

Who are you?

Have you ever asked
yourself this question?

You might answer by saying:

"I am tall."
"I am from New York."

Or...?

How would you answer?

But is that who **YOU** are?

Or are those just descriptions?

You might also answer by saying:

"I like dancing."
"I don't like trying new foods."

Or...?

How would you answer?

But is that who **YOU** are?

Or are those just likes and dislikes?

You might even answer by saying:

"I'm the best at math!"
"I'm not the greatest at soccer."

Or...?

How would you answer?

But is that who YOU are?

Or are those just thoughts?

You are not your thoughts.

You are not your likes and dislikes.

You are not the things you worry about,
or even the things you believe.

So, if you are not those things...

Who are you?

Did you know there's something that can help you discover who you are?

It's called *mindfulness*.

Mindfulness is something you can practice anytime, anywhere.

Mindfulness is a way of being *here right now.*

Mindfulness brings you to what's *real and true.*

It brings you to who you *already are.*

It brings you
HERE.

It brings you into the
NOW.

Some people think mindfulness is...

about getting rid of thoughts,
which would actually be impossible because you have thousands and thousands of thoughts every day.

about always being calm,
which would get boring after a while because you'd miss out on getting excited, or laughing your head off, or letting yourself be really sad because it's been a hard day.

about fixing yourself to be perfect, which wouldn't even make sense because "perfect" means something different to everyone anyway.

only for certain people, which isn't true—mindfulness is for anyone and everyone!

Mindfulness is about *remembering*.

So what are we actually remembering?

Who
we
truly
are.

As we practice mindfulness we might:

feel less anxious,
sleep better,
feel calm,
be more at ease.

That's pretty cool!

And there's even more that's possible.

Like finding out what is **real** and **true** about life.

And finding out what is **real** and **true** about yourself.

So, how do we practice mindfulness?

First we begin by **learning something really awesome...**

You can put your attention

where you want it to be.

Have you ever heard an adult say,

"Pay attention!"

Did they say it in a nice way?
Did they even tell you *how* to do it?

Being mindful *isn't* a drag.
It's *not* a chore.

Think about how you pay attention to something you love. Paying attention mindfully can be like that. It can be like paying attention to a puppy, or a friend.

Or...

What do you love?

Mindfulness is about putting your attention where **you** want it...

instead of feeling out of control,
or like your thoughts are the boss of you.

And there's an extra bonus...

When it comes to mindfulness, there's no judging, no grades, just kindness. Isn't that a relief?

You can't do this wrong.

And an *extra super-duper* bonus...

As we keep our attention here and now,
we remember what's **real** and **true**...

You can *be* with whatever *is.*

You can be with anger.
You can be with excitement.
You can be with sadness.
You can be with joy.

You are like the space of a cup that can hold whatever gets poured in.

But...

if your attention is on *yesterday*,

you might forget.

And if your attention is on *tomorrow,*

you might forget.

And that's not bad or wrong.
Just know that you've got options.
You can mindfully bring your attention
back **HERE** and **NOW**.

And then sprinkle it with kindness.
Just 'cause you can.

And, because kindness is what's real.

*(Plus, meanness doesn't help
anyone or anything. Ever.)*

So...

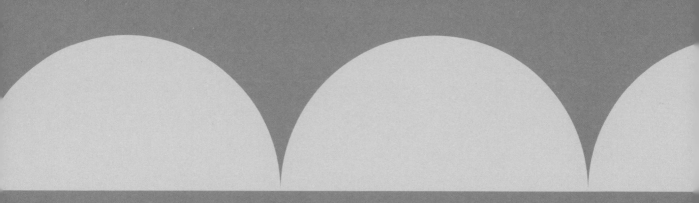

What are you noticing in your mind

right now?

Here's a secret...**YOU** are already great at living in the now.

It's something kids are naturally in touch with—being in the moment.

Which is really cool because the only thing that's *actually real* is **NOW**.

Is there *actually* anything
other than NOW?

Have you ever *actually* left NOW
to go to the past?

Have you ever been in
a real time machine?

Have you ever traveled to this thing
we call the future?

How would you even do this?

IT'S *ALWAYS* NOW!

Have you ever noticed adults often get stuck thinking about the future or the past?

Worried about what will happen tomorrow, or regretting something that happened a long time ago?

It can be so normal, they forget that the whole thing—the always feeling bad about the past and future...

is optional!

It's easy to forget that the adults around you used to be young. That they, perhaps, lived in *the now* with more ease.

Sometimes in the whole growing-up thing, people feel like they need to put on masks.

They start pretending.

Have YOU ever felt like this?

Have you ever felt like you couldn't be yourself, or like you should act a certain way to make someone else happy?

Or that you had to hide your feelings?

What is up
with that?

Sometimes we're afraid to be ourselves.

We try to change ourselves.
We try to be different than we are.

But actually, the *safest* place to be is...

OURSELVES.

Not the self who
  is tall,
  is not that great at soccer,
  likes math,
  worries about the future,
  tries to be different...

but the **real self** that
you know in your bones.

The one that mindfulness
helps you remember.

How do you know this real self?

Through **being**.
Just as you are.

You ARE
loved,
whole,
worthy,
enough,
authentic,
naturally
curious,

inherently accepting, beyond time, beyond space, infinite!

Who you are is SO much bigger than any thought, any mask, any belief, any fear, any...*anyTHING!*

When you know who you are
you tend to feel confident, unstoppable,
grounded, at ease—but not because
you've aced a test, or made your
grownups happy, or given the "right"
answer, or made a good joke.

Mindfulness helps you get in touch with something deeper than this.

Mindfulness helps you remember who you are when no one is watching, when you aren't comparing yourself to anyone else, when you are simply BEING.

This is where happiness lives.

In your very BEING.

In yourself.

Even though hard things will happen, it helps to remember that you might feel sadness, or hurt, or anger about this hard thing. But...

YOU are not this hard thing.

YOU aren't that sadness.
YOU aren't that hurt.
YOU aren't that anger.

Sadness is actually happening **IN** you.
Hurt rises up **IN** you.
Anger passes **THROUGH** you.

Imagine an open sky...

There might be fluffy clouds.
There might be storm clouds.
There might be birds, or lightning, or planes.
They all pass through the same open sky.

Does whatever passes through
the sky *change* the sky?

No, the sky is always here.
It doesn't change.

You are like that.

And if you forget, what can help you remember the **NOW**?

What can help you remember **YOU**?

The breath.

What's so awesome about the breath?

It is always **here** and **now**.

So give it a go. Try it now.

Breathe.

Can you feel your breath coming
in and out of your *nose*?
Or your *belly*?
Or your *chest*?

Try counting each breath
and see if you can get up to 10.

Once you're at 10, start again at 1.

How do you
you feel?

What do you
notice?

Enjoy the breath.

Be here now and remember
who you are.

Because *this* is the safe place.

How is that possible?

Because this safe space is **YOU**.

Your very **BEING**.

Anxiety, sadness, anger,
or fear can arise in **YOU**.

Anything can arise in you.

Everything arises in you.

And all of it is OK.

YOU have room for all of it.

YOU are the empty cup.

YOU are the open sky.

YOU are yourself.

Outro
for grownups

Happiness is the very nature of our being. Mindfulness can help us discover this. It can help us remember.

It's easy to feel lost in a world that sometimes doesn't value who we truly are. In our confusion about who we are we tend to struggle. Our confusion leads to disharmony. Kids deserve to be supported in exploring their inner landscape—as do grownups. Hopefully, this book plants a seed of awakening in such a way that you, and the kid you're reading with can share a direct experience of who we really are. We can assist our kids in discovering who they are when we embark on this discovery for ourselves.

Mindfulness isn't woo-woo. Neither is it an escape. We all long to be happy. Through this journey, we can cultivate greater harmony—not only within ourselves, but with each other and in the world. Our happiness and our freedom become possible through such exploration.

May your journey be a rich and fulfilling discovery. May you know yourself as the peace and happiness you long for.

About The Author

Caverly Morgan (she/her) wrote this book for young people who enjoy asking big questions. And she wrote *The Heart of Who We Are: Realizing Freedom Together* for grownups who like to ask big questions. Her own question-asking included 8 years of training in a silent Zen monastery.

Caverly experiences life through the teachings of Zen and nonduality—seeing everything as part of one whole, rather than separated by difference. She uses both approaches to teach people that we are all made of the same stuff and that we all inherently belong.

She believes that lasting change starts within and is passionate about personal and collective transformation. Caverly delights in connecting with people of all ages and believes everyone deserves to be supported in asking big questions and deeply exploring the heart of who we are.

 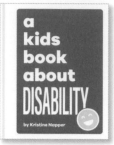  

  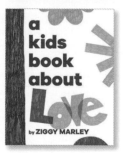 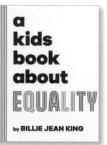 
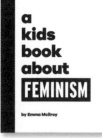  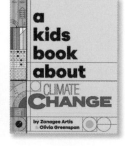 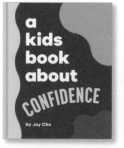